BLACK MUSIC, POLITICS, AND WORD BOMBS

ORLANDO TAYLOR

PUBLISHER

Web of Ananse Publishing

USA

Black Music, Politics, and Word Bombs

Copyright © 2023 by Orlando Taylor
Library of Congress Control Number: 2023909395

All rights reserved. Printed in the United States of America. No part of this book may be used or reproduced in any manner whatsoever without written permission except for brief quotations embodied in critical articles or reviews.

This book is a work of fiction. Names, characters, businesses, organizations, places, events, and incidents either are the product of the author's imagination or are used fictitiously. Any resemblance to actual persons, living or dead, events, or locales is entirely coincidental.

For information contact:
theteam@kuumbaconcepts.com

Publisher: Web of Ananse Publishing
Editor: Laura Brown
Cover Design: Nduka Abii
Cover Concept/Illustrations: Orlando Taylor
ISBN: 979-8-9882122-0-1
ISBN: 979-8-9882122-1-8 (eBook)
First Edition: June 2023

9 8 7 6 5 4 3 2 1

Table of Contents

DEDICATION

The book is dedicated to my mother, Velma CeWilla Osborne-Taylor, who raised me and gave me all she had so I could become all that I am. It is also dedicated to my niece, Amaris Chew, who died in a car accident but had nothing but the greatest love and encouragement for her uncle. Love you both. And finally, to my brothers and sisters who are a part of my work as they are a part of me.

BLACK MUSIC, POLITICS, AND WORD BOMBS

INTRODUCTION

Since the coronavirus pandemic hit the planet, it feels like the veil between reality and what one's mind wants to process began to deteriorate quickly. Even for me, it felt unbelievable, like a valve had been opened to release decades of pressure.

But would it be enough to move the country and the world to a better place socio-politically? The world's lowest levels of people began to see politicians, oligarchs, and celebrities of all types in a more honest light. Independent online information sources and social media became lightning rods for challenging the accuracy of news outlets and pundits, despite corporations operating to the contrary. It is powerful and important, and I wanted to be a part of this.

The death of George Floyd on May 25, 2020, in real-time, left a loud silence concerning life in the United States for people who are descendants of enslaved Africans. The knee on the neck of the black community is real and powerful, like a bomb going off in the middle of our best dream.

In the words I use to address my feelings and thoughts, I am not proposing any particular solutions to these controversial issues. However, I have learned that saying nothing nor doing anything has ever been a part of a plan for a better society.

Reading the poems may be difficult because it renders images of things we don't like to think about. Still, I hope they add to the clarity of your own emotions and desires about these topics. A period to your complex thoughts and experiences.

So many individuals and organizations are doing great work to address all kinds of issues that permeate the black community. However, I wanted to add my screams of passion and quips about what it all means to me and what I think it means to us. I hope the next four score-plus pages will rock you, awaken you, confirm you, console you and affirm what you feel is real.

Afrike

K. Frimpong & His Cubano Fiestas/ Kyenkyen Bi Adi Mawu

Afrike, I did not want to leave you
Dragged my feet on the shores
Dug my fingers deep
into your creation spirit
They carried me away chained in boats
Screaming louder than a newborn
for his mother's nipples
No matter the song
I know your melody
Gave my life its meaning
In a reality devoid of your juju
The drum's rhythm could not traverse
So, we had to make new ones
I cannot count the years I was made blind
Loving you was a crime
they sold us for dimes
Excommunicated from humanity
They laugh at their own beginning
The foundation is not enough

Ancestors in my psyche
Poked my soul to wokeness
I see even when I am deaf
Your music turns the mountains into speakers
The baobab tree dances
All the planet knows your vocals
Rushing to have your herbs heal this world
Precious history in my blood

Steal a ram's horns before
they can take the history of my people
I jump like the Maasai
at the chance to speak to you
A wind unhindered by manmade things
With the speed of two-year-old legs
meeting baba at the door
Like a little kid screaming during jump rope
I swim with the people
lost first through bondage
A fire that burns only energies
that seek to destroy us all
Atlantic take me back
Atlantic teleport me back to Africa
I am going, going back, back to Africa
Afrike will protect me
Eshu at the crossroads
Orunmila make weapons to see us safe
Olu, pound your foot on the heads of enemies
those who try to make Afrike their sacrifice
In err, this world is only for their life
Afrike may my head
know your lap after the fight

All Hail Dinknesh

Kwaku Asante /AWOL/honeycomb

Disdain on your membrane
For the children of Dinknesh
You got game we gave you the rules
Everything rained down from Kemet
Aid to your existence
What's at the source of this spiritual schism
False definitions in stereo
Digested quicker than milk and cereal
Africans embraced enlightenment
Over de jure destruction
Society's definition is nothing without us
Drinking nectar from her cups
Adoration for her self-creation
Conjured the first man
Allowed you to grow up with hue-mans
Using your hands to choke our grandmother
We raise ours in praise

Using her magic with surgical skill
Splicing neutrons at the quantum level
Mitosis and meiosis into villages
Each with its own mission
Ensuring continuance
Universal purpose fills the soul
Foundation to all existence
Snicker from on the other sides of cages
At the mountainous hips that bore us all
Circus of pure contempt

Swoop like vultures pecking our culture
I hear her now more than ever
A scream from out of time
Waking our minds to all we forgot
Trapped in our DNA nothing was missing
I know you feel it
A prickling on your neck
When you hear her say, Get up!

Ancestors Raise Gods

Kojey Radical/Kwame Nkrumah

They look at me the god I should be
still thinking it's about niggas and guns
Infused with blessed feminine energy
Forced to see the god in me
ever since I stored scrolls in my chest
Movement to movement
living my jazz composition
I am no jarhead
desperate to be led soul-dier
High priest in my own religion,
more blasphemy and heresy the better
Melchizedek, I knew him
Sweet smell like sharp cheddar
Plethora of unreal philosophies
giving me the hebegebees
Bless Orunmila I am not easily fooled
Breaking down bullshit at lightspeed
Past lives in Kmt and Atlantis as a scientific priest
Preparation for living beyond the tenth millennium

Ancestors haunt my dreams
There is no reason for hesitation
Proof positive I am lasting undone
See the god, your eyes fear in me
Still thinking it's only about niggas with guns
It's the nectar of your soul,
Excellence made living
Purified shield against hate

Ancestors haunt my dreams
Freeing them I have become the embodiment
of ancestral prophecies, and the sweet taste
of my father's tears made real
They look at me the god I should be
Still thinking it's about niggas and guns
Infused with blessed feminine energy
Forced to see the god in myself
Ever since I stored scrolls in my chest
Movement to movement
Living my jazz composition
I am the sweet taste of my father's tears

Anger

Teebs / Moments

Don't let it strangle me,
gum in life's keyhole
Clogging turns left and right
Emptying of false understanding saved me
Righteous anger overflowing my sea
Like bags of sand failing on the Mississippi

Cattle feed normalcy
Weight hotter than the August sun
Never to be useless and inept
With life's mucous in my chest

Leaves falling have no choice
Oya's winds cleanse the heart
Avoiding spiritual, ventricle aorta hardening
Bolted souls cannot accept

Emptying false understanding saved me
Righteous anger overtakes me
Comfortable in the presence of mine own deity
Your shadow is shorter than my journey
No one can steal what the Ancestors gifted

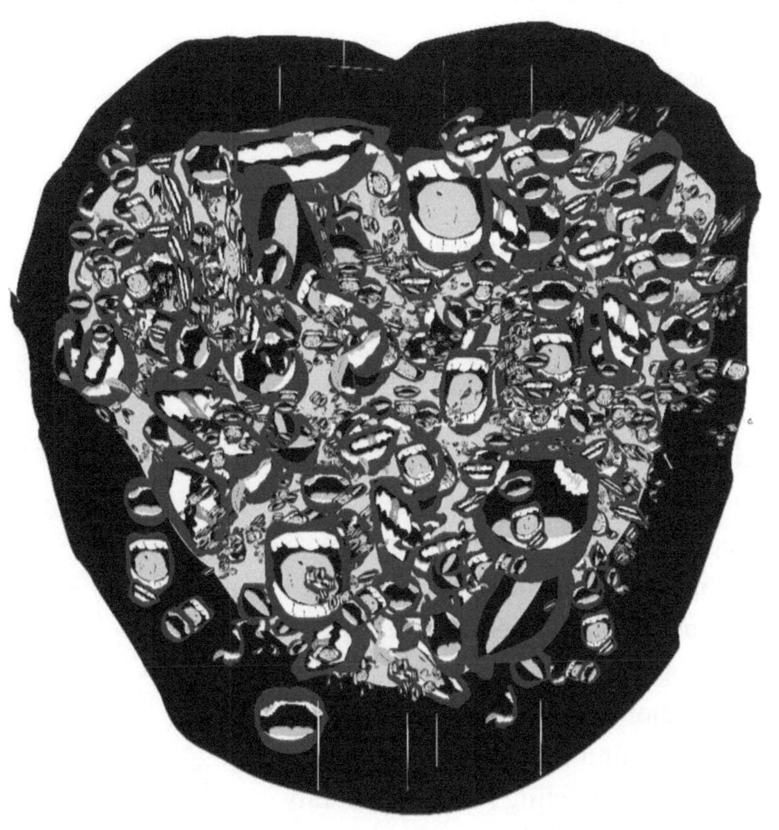

Balance

Branford Marsalis/ Beautyful Ones Are Not Yet Born

Negative energy on all sides
Clouds cover the sun like a tomb
Mothers cut out their uterus
in world protest
Governments bent on vacating humanity
But we all want a family
since we going to the Mars
Corporations dine on a mixture of dreams,
hope, and citizen's blood
brought to you by debilitated leaders
And hypnotic ads from corporations
in search of their own fake freedom news
Ten-year-old girls become brides to the past
Night goes to war against the day
We accept the unquestioned true intent
Tie a string around the hand of an uneducated man
Makes it easy for him to pull the lever
Closing arrogantly on life's scene
Hope is a fathomless meme
Do you see the future in a child's laughter?
Everyday people erecting local community
Channeling echoes of uhuru
Karmic snap back to acts
thought hidden from the heavens
Awareness becoming more common
Youth throw away destructive traditions
Black woman's wisdom is healing this earth
No expectations or sunlight banned

Truthful expression of the life you are living

Baptized in The Fire on Vinegrove

Black Milk/Perfected on Puritan Ave.

Baptized into existence on Vinegrove
Hotter than an August summer
Pop Sanders screaming, cutting lil' peanut heads
Caldwell swears all her kids good
Did you see what the twins did?
Amen local minister beating his kids
Praise and screams of pain intermingle
A potent ying-yang melody escaping their lips

House of chaos adjacent to my reality
Nightmares melted into my day
Visions of child abandonment
Fighting family in the rain,
did your soul come clean?
Matriarch defines dark meanness
Concerned no farther than grandchildren's fed check
Charles cut his wrist
Looked like a vampire offering eternal life
a deluge of blood poured down his forehead
Dear God, I wonder if you'd
come to save me

Our block, an eclectic mass of housing
No cookie cutters, but all homes
Sonny's clean Delta 88
Prettier than Holmes' white Toronado
She got a Lincoln Town car every other year
Dream of owning Grime's mansion
Filled with hope for a better station
Graduations bring American
dreams close like a telescope
Living our hopes in success for the children

A malaise of racism in St. Louis,
prevented many from becoming
exploding in their magic
Lives torn down by drugs
planted by Ronald Reagan
Sacrificed our neighborhoods
on the altar of fake democracy
and Manifest Destiny

Better Than Good

(For black men who don't see their beauty)
Mannywellz/So Good

Feel your energy
a Yoruba dance
the drum
undulating with you
One, one rhythm
your taut neck muscles
encompassed by mahogany rings
Painted face fierce in our West Africa tradition
Frescos of black with reds, tan
and bronze layered with violet and green
Hard corners of your jaw
reflection of character and empathy
Stark thick skin perfect
for sweet moist kisses
Cracked with life's moments
Soft, wet like new cotton
dipped in dew
Mouth, mean like a flower
pushing hard to bloom
Protecting the sunlight in your smile
Caress that scowl that
whites convinced you was ugly
Eyes black reflecting
the depths of existence
Portal to your micro verse
a mirror of her heaven
Allow another brother

Rest his weary head on your rough shoulder
He's more than a brother
Simultaneously your baby
Chunky wide nose
for a nibble and maybe an earring
Stop the King Kong
There is no monkey in
the code of your creation
Braid twist lock press plait natural curl
from the softest to four c
Many combinations of a theme
Connect wires and antennae
see if we can find some other aliens
The body they tear at
both envied and lusted for
Is not the foundation of your godhood
But a beautiful extension
of your inner juju
I give you my tears of joy, admiration
and pride as a fragrance
To keep their hate from corrupting
your godlike aroma

Black Man Dance

Dance
Get on those black toes
Reach for Oya with your souls
The stars are yours
Loosen the body
Flail against the tropes of maleness
Brokenness is not only yours
Sunlight on your faces
Piece of passion
a bird in hand
A peace of land,
Silences the mind

Dance
Spread denied wings
Create gales and forceful winds
Twirl like a tornado
Sango take hold
transform into a firenado
Like nature you create anew
Ain't no move you won't imagine
Ain't no move you can't animate
Remove white supremacy,
barriers cock blocking juju

Dance
Fantastical gymnastic feats
Make them hate you complete

Don't make life an enemy
Make it tinkle
piano keys played lightly
watch Stevie
Walk with a limp
right amount of arrogance
In tandem dip roll twerk
Stomp into oblivion that
which is contrary to your existence
Improvisational jazz moves
They are incapable of understanding
how to write you coherently

Dance
Transatlantic African slave trade
Left ley lines of energy
Gifted us power a plenty
Here it comes building, educating,
ushering sisters and brothers
to the best wisdom
Older than ten thousand BCE
Atlantis is on the left coast of the continent
Not fairytales of white people underwater
Myths got me pop-locking in laughter
Like b-boys, spin on your backs
Then hold your nuts at them
Dance to the rhythm of
who you know you are
Show them everything
their petrified you'd be
Dance
Pleasing only the god
reflected in the prism

of your existence

Dance
Dance
Dance
Black man,
Dance

Black Pride

Kabaka Pyramid / Free from Chains

Always talking about agenda
Cash seems to be the goal
All up and down American islands
Not to mention the Rastas
Dem sale big dick for mammon
To old fat white women
crashing airplanes to get dem drops
Without the gehs you murder
the negative black man's image
you never fought

More than neck rolls, finger pops,
and frozen vogue poses
Ancient priests, medicine men
Say Harlem Renaissance without us
Incredible didactic thinkers
We stay teaching lessons to yo' kids
Godlike creativity
Can't reduce us to fag
A spiritual assault, sin
A purposeful gaff

Black, I say lead
There'll be no kowtowing pirouettes
Eye rolls, waiting on you to decide
We gwan be more than alive
Thrive no matter the style
Nothing but the truth of us beguiles

Appearing as needed
The balance dictated by Her creation
So why you hatin' on your brothers
Maat will not allow you to lie
Our existence is not at risk

Blues of Blackness

The Souljazz Orchestra / Celestial Blues

Blackness blue as Ma Rainey
belting truths about Manifest Destiny
Land mines everywhere I step
I get a little smaller
the more of my soul gets blown away
Most hated on the planet
Mad cause we the most
Monetized access to my own culture
Picking bones like the vulture
Love the music
Our dance
the embodiment of heaven's hosts
Our tones made the first falling stars
An angelic response to our call
For a time, we partied with demigods

But they preferred the aroma of death
Gurgles of drowning black bodies
in the ocean devoid of passion
Screaming as mothers beg
for their black pearls
being tossed to alligators as bait
Human wind chimes
Swinging from baobab trees
Lashes cracking like cooking fires
Raped from sun up to sun down
Bagging souls with cotton for sale
Scraps fall from white men's teeth

down at our feet
Symphony played for Judaism,
Christianity, and Islam are all conductors,
DS Al Coda back at the beginning

White supremacy smells the ending
Nineteen sixties movie scenes
Dogs replaced with tasers and tear gas
Batons transformed into mech suits
Cars transform to robotic slave catchers
Officer Friendly was a plant
Only citizens who have been bombed
Every corner we turn there's a gate
Afraid to let us escape
Mediocre and desperate
Idea faucet dry like porridge
TikTok stats ain't a lie
Only way you survive
Forced into birth
With bated breath we see demons
Escape punishment
While our limbs ache
Hanging from political trees
Fruit rotting before it falls
Nothing new comes from its seeds
Somehow in nature
We are the enemy

Celebrity Conversation

Pharoah Monch /Rapid Eye Movement

History in America
called the black atrocities
Pain and brutality meted out
Biggest heist in human history
Inventions of psychotic psychedelic
imperialist delusions
Blueprint to worldwide soul-ransom
Ever seen Leopold's rubber mansion
Billions profited off vaccines
synthesized from Henrietta Lacks's genes
Can't be free and don't want you to stay
A conundrum for the neanderthal
Black celebrities are tangent
to white supremacy
Endure indentured servitude
Exchanged for the flashing lights
Adoration just to be an object
as they travel to space
Using your tired knotted back
As a resting place for their feet
Created a legacy by selling
your great-grandmother's dreams
No returns all sales final
Possessing your soul is absolute
Got your forty acres guarantee
The freedom you attained
bought chains for your people
Master's orders lead droves into a fire

Grin, act, dance, catch, shoot that ball
Sing caged bird, sing
Transfiguration into any character
you can imagine
Except an African unafraid of living

Covenant of Not Belonging

John Coltrane / Blue Train

They built a wall for us
Denied applications to
middle-class sensation
Erased our past with a barrel of laughs
Substituted a fake news narrative
This was our beginning
Our existence here
the result of someone else's sin
Gave us American Negro civilization
As they stumbled over Atlantis
Stuttered pronouncing Kemet
Repetition cleanses your mind
Black folks eat their historical preaching
Afrique's languages sing when we speak
Their speech is like boulders
crashing into a piano
Perversion of our humanity
We understand us better in song
Coerced into dawning a
cloak of erased culture
A super-powered telepathic mind control
American music, dance,
is black African language,
at its most creative and moving
elegant anger with forthrightness
of the well written episodes
from the Africans in America
Bent like a dope fiend

we miss the curtain call
Against their laws
To clap for them, ceases all efforts
No humans involved remember
White supremacy dropped a bomb
Like the MOVE organization
Sankofa will save us

Painful Beautiful Space

Bob Marley & Wailers/Three Little Birds

Singing like the wind
racing among the trees
Wolf baying in the night
to a family in chorus
Hymns of a black man
fishing to feed his babies
Melody of the sea
lapping lullabies
on rocks and white shores
Wondrous sound
beating in my ears
Breathing with stones
in my chest,
my stress
The first drums and dance
echoing toil and
joys of living
Swelling in my being
fatter than big mama's ankles
into a painful beautiful space

Dance without shame
or embarrassment
A salve on my skin
Oshun's waters
A queen's quick step
on her seventh birthday
Three steps of sorrow

when a black boy
loses his baba
Bob your head
jerk your neck back
to hard labor
endured for love
Your steps flutter
like a bird's
landing wings
Peace from white supremacy
a salsa dance of passion
changing tempos,
key signatures
Death to emotional sobriety
Death to emotional sobriety
Swelling from life's trauma
transforming the uneven tears
in our interrupted hopes
into a beautiful painful space

Faggot

Rukus/Pour Me Water (Slave)

Eddie gave it long
when he came to town
Whole network of churches
Glad handling him
Michael Peterson dancing
with his white beefcakes

Faggot

Music execs signing checks
while molesting artists
Make the ladies die for you
First fellatio my nuts
Altar boys praying to Catholic obelisks
Worldwide system raping boys
Passed around the islands
rife with Papal tenderness
Like Thomas Jefferson
dragging Sally Hemmings

Faggot

Lindsey out here catching
a hundred thousand grams
from men online
Lady G paying tonight!
Burly American wrestlers
succeed as entertainers

if they stripper dance
upside down on a ladder
Shouts and prayers to my black IG models
Slash trainer, slash actor, slash doctor,
slash barber, slash Cashapp me
and I'll show my ass
Ninety-five percent of your posts
abs and thighs they're grrrreat!

Faggot, faggot, faggot

Family stab me in daylight
Switchblade of sharp words,
old dick in the booty as nigga
shroud of shame like Tourin
is all you gave
Cut for eight seconds
Where's my memory,
he's bisexual
Fear in me driven out
by the hypocrisy,
y'all hypocrisy
and my godhood evolution

Faggot?

Queen Tings

Burna Boy/Another Story

Queen of slavery
Queen of blood
Queen of all things brutal
Blood on your hands
starched monarch standing over the world
Indigenous people of Canada replaced
with scrubbed clones of themselves
Guyana destabilized and parceled out
to the IMF and World Bank
Caribbean extension of the continent

Working millions of Africans into oblivion
on sugarcane and banana plantations
Profits stuffed in UK's brassiere
Ugandan cotton land grabs
sucked the soil dry
Death to 11,000 Mau Mau
A nightmare of the Kikuyu
Displaced in their own homeland
Malawi became an Imperial slum
Drowned in tea and tobacco leaves
Nyasaland never accepted Rhodesia
White sister grafted in
No gold in Gambia but
groundnuts from South America
became its lifeblood

Yoruba, Hausa, and Igbo

sewn into a patchwork quilt of fire
devour each other, and not their enemy
Organized into violence
not their common interests
Passed around like a fútbol
Dutch, Portuguese, France, Britain
Abolition of slavery had Mauritius
filled with stolen Indians and Chinese
Australia, just shy of Turtle Island
A planned penal colony
Over a million aboriginals
dumped into the sea so
it could be a beach resort
For the Windsor's people

Queen of slavery
Queen of blood
Queen of all things brutal
Reveled in our oppression
Wearing our culture and resources
in a sick cosplay

Nigeria
Uganda
Australia
Nyasaland
Malawi
Gambia
Canada
Belize
Bahamas
Mauritius
Jamaica
India
Papua New Guinea
Mau Mau
Solomon Islands
Grenada
Antigua and Barbuda

You're Mine

James Blake /I Mind

You're Mine
I mind
Who you see
What time the place to be
Decisions you make
for our sake
Watching so you
step through so fine
You got my hands and
back to help you climb
Loyalty and dedication
are the zodiac signs
Before we stack any funds
build the proper spiritual energy
we can grill

You're Mine
I mind
How the family treats you
and if they see your reality
Your path and being is just as divine
Rage is the only emotion I retain
If they spit on your crown
Mitigate the wellspring
of broken promises
and false meditations
Cast a spell to undo
hateful revelations

Choose an instrument
and avoid the sedatives
Your shadow is brighter
than their reflection

I mind
Yes, I mind
You're Mine

First God
Alfa Mist / Potential

Woman, Black
since the beginning
your energy willed
things into existence
Human life begins feminine
You too my strong black
masculine intelligent alpha male
a real nigga's, Nigga
Were once a strong
black woman before the signal
to your tran-sition
Giiiirrrl

Black woman
your being is a wonder
Crafting and cradling
into a new god humanity
You echo the universe
on a micro level
Contracting and expanding simultaneously
Mystified, with what's to come
Ancient obelisk first dildo
trying to fuck the sky
A cloudless understanding
it takes energy of the earth
and universe to create Ife

Black woman
Be at peace
You are the immeasurable,
mathematical permutation,
twelve times checked computation,
of all we need you to be
Time began with you
And it will cease without you
There is no story of the world
that is interesting
and breath-stealing
devoid of your existence

Black woman,
the promise and prophecy,
I pledge on my momma,
my first God
now convened
with the Ancestors,
that you are the world
the universe is texting about
from planet to planet

Honor Her

Lil Simz/Heart on Fire

Standing up against
all kinds of turmoil
Men with too many children
by outside women
Raped to save our dignity
She continues to burn and keep us whole
and bore children for massa
she had hard times seeing
A true feminist maintaining her womanhood
Whilst fighting for freedom in multiple ways
Raising seeds to proper gods
even when love and respect
has waned by the father
Your mad cause she actually accomplished
what you said you were gonna do?
The guv-ment didn't stop Tulsa, Rosewood,
East St. Louis from existing
Tearing off my shirt and unleashing
That dirty, uncaring, glaring,
fuck your whole existence personality
Aiming an automatic .45 as best I can
At every word meant to beat
and stuff the first God into a gourd
Your words and ways are robbers of
spiritual cosmic purpose
Speak carefully, I'm by the door
a casket is the only way you departing
if these are the teachings you're imparting

Blessed respect to her name
Shouldering the conscience
of the true origin in her universe
It's crucial to get yo' iwa réré
the best it can be
No complaints
You have been honored
the embodiment of all things African
my brother throughout our history

No Phobias

Pharoah Monch /Triskaidekaphobia

Envy filled people
mumbling adjectives
death under their breath
Judging my canvas
wisdom about life
with another man's
decoder ring
Now I'm mean?!
Can't absorb the low vibration
bullets you spitting
Walk the ways
of the Ancestors
Probability high it
makes me a rebel
Gnashing your teeth
tongue on the floor
Anger misplaced
no words to say
I'm an unabridged dictionary
something different everyday
a butterfly crossed with a god
Heart forged from a star
Mind touched by Imhotep healing
Katwe molded a mystical warrior
Culture a cloak of protection
A holy cycle you'll see me again

Da da da dang
Da da da dang
Messing with a nine
you lack the brains
Da da da dang
Da da da dang
Now *you're* afraid,
catch game

Live

Bob Marley & Wailers/ Wake and Live

When the portal to the world
is on the representation
of your preservation
Though some advised you to run
subscribe to your roots an
inflection making you stand
Like the oldest
trees in Alkebulan

Live

No matter the time
or the incarnation
of coded workplace masks
Tardiness of mind and spirit
are always assigned
Expected mediocrity a key
for microaggressions
and a silent fuck you
Create a cataract glaze
donut of your mind
Say the incantation to
clear the ghosts
picking at your mind

Live

Never satisfied with

the work of the nines
never willing to pay
more than a dime
Baldwin told you nigger
Is not a part of our kind
African culture is on the line
Silence befalls the earth
Once we are gone
Our ancestors twerked to
the joy of the rising sun

Live

Respect the wisdom in your father
Honor the god in your sister
Pan-Africanism's mirror in place
Reflection, melanated skin
same throughout the Diaspora
Ancestor's teachings
binding us across
the multiverse
Transatlantic holocaust created
an alternate timeline
I spray my juju on all Ethiops
May completeness be
untouchable wealth
as long as you shun your roots

Live

Into the Sun 'til Done

Jorga Smith / Gone

Boy you gon' die
settin' in sun
Can survive the center of a star?
Purified in the mouth of Rhe
Arise a better useful power
Improve the probability
of my forever existence
Confirm my devotion
to the black resistance
Skin burned dark as
the universe
Blinding radiance
a concert removing
the blues embedded
in my future
Dive into the sun's deep end
Peace in energy
Begin all endings
Halt all beginnings
Taste sun ray espressos
with quantum toast
Bursting with the flavor
of a prophecy fulfilled
A person meant to be
like light rising in the creases
of my people's skin

Misfit to Cornerstone

Saba / Busy Sirens

Born at the beginning of a new era
coinciding with the death of a King
Promise upon promise spat in black people's face
Black folks living zombie lives in the day
gods of desire and purpose in the night

Hot summer night
sweltering humidity
thicker than racism
Fat rats bent on devouring me
I was screaming in the language
only a mother can decipher
Saved from the hereafter
to live in the ever after
At a quarter of a score
ran over by a car
on Labadie and Newstead Ave
Unscathed save a scarred chin
Head and soul intact
Ancestors shields at one hundred percent
Suicide was once a choir
I listened to with deep desire
Hated myself for a moment
not recognizing the movements

I'd been gifted
Shame was my calling
from mundane family
A weakness, psoriasis
on the skin of realness
Nearly eaten as a youth
by one who was sure
my body was his to consume
Allergic reaction
to healing an ocular infection
ravage my body and
damaged my cloak of melanin
Death knocking like a demon
serving an arrest warrant
one hundred four degrees Fahrenheit
three days straight
Doctor told Mudear to call my daddy
before the angles
turned the lights off
Life for this little black
nerd boy was up

Now I'm beyond surviving
Floating on the energy
gifted by the Orishas of Ifá
Understanding how it's
consistently been there
putting a cornerstone
where it meant to be

Speaking through me like bold prophets
Destined, strong, proclaimed
an existence sang about to the stars
Cast off despair, toss the doubt
into the ocean of the bygone
It has no place with the juju
they have bestowed

Sands of Time

Teebs/Bound Ball

Dancing on the sands of time
Thought they had a cage
to silence a mind
Unbound by your
perceptions of excellence
Life is its own definition
Being is this torrid orgasm
Body convulsing
at every tick to life's pop
Coming up dandelion
the true ghetto rose
Overstand facts
leave nothing to suppose
Mind is a universe times eight
Orunmila's hammered creation
Its deep in the African essence
The quantum physics of human existence
Dancing on the sands of time
Adjusting your thought process
Quench your visions
You need meditation
Be in full possession of the soul
Never lose your mind
Mind of my mind
Parables of the Sower
Sands of time

make droplets of memories
for all the Moorish children
connected to the
Dream papyrus

I'm a terrorist

Nas / Rare

Enduring destruction of the architects
of Manifest Destiny
Legal way of enemies pretends to be heroes
Mediocrity needs a proper fade
The synchronized imploding entities
sucking the teat of Alkebulan
Forced their entry into
the treasure of its uterus
like sex worker with broken legs
forced to service a racist
Erectile dysfunction of the
UN, Catholic Corp, IMF,
World Bank, Peace Corps, WHO
a poisonous alphabet stew
Salt turning souls into dried meat
All they look to do is break
Euro complains the world is teetering
crumbs you left
History riddle with meteor showers
Indentations forced penetration
deep inside indigenous existence

You shudder in disbelief
My righteous fantasy
Dive bomb a plane
into the White House
and Mt. Rushmore
Landmines line the floor

at the NY Stock Exchange
Strangle Belgium with Congo's
rubber bands
Speak a spell to make cocoa
turn you loco
Stab the British crown in the heart
Arrogantly take back our art
Disconnect the Francophone
Pay your illegal fees to make a call
Deutschland idiots thought
they could conjure the perfect human
Science said not without melanin
Hurl a nuclear spear
to the country's court
Take a tiki torch to Buckingham Palace
House of ill-repute
And perverted imaginings
of a frog prince
All the darkness associated with
the existence of white supremacy
Never get them moral naps straight
no matter how hot the comb gets
Karma has you in her arms
French kissing you into poverty
Dreams filled with your screams
Set to a drum-symphony

Let's Get Powerful

Life demands change
A shard of how nature operates
Fighting against immutable facts is useless
God energy spilt on the floor
Like seed guarded from a paid whore

Are you the only one who's seen
Black boys get jumped for chump change
Did you live next to an unknown demon
Brutalizing black young gods
left in supposed loving care
Only to grow up in a living horror show
Black pearl girl screams
quieted with a fellatio ending
Her brother, to us both
can't see or hear me
Cast a spell to forget
erasure of our brotherhood
and love to crystallize a shield
made upon Orunmila's anvil
He is forever lost to me
dug out the memories to alleviate his pain

I see you brother
A reflection in our memory DNA
and the everyday
Anger and lack of knowledge are not an excuse

for a pause in movement
Going against your nature
You are always the fiercest warrior
when in pursuit of deep understanding
of people and the environment around them
Fred Hampton didn't raise one gun
at white supremacy
But his Meter Neter fueled by his wisdom
Got him gunned down by an army
Understand that
So, get up and let's get powerful

Dope Everyday People

Rapsody / Serena

Everyday people
Existing near the beginning
Living mean
Not silver-filled mouths
Whip marks and torture
not spared cause you switching
Honest path as any man
Sharecroppers bending ag-science
Grinding knuckles to produce
sweet-potatoes
Building families into homes
Served wars with all the boys
Hiding behind burlap
and medals no more
Dreaming of sunsets
fantasy we can only see
Porters immaculate
in presentation
Writers beyond the soft light
of a dying stars life
Teachers opening minds
to the possibilities
you did not envision
Ministers ushering
spirit into a better energy
No priesthood excluded
Canvas of our souls
painted with indelible colors

of our blood
Singing songs stolen from
the Nephilim
Now you know why
you can't stop listening
Roll our hopes and future in paper
smoke this life to euphoria

Black Boy Juju

Jada Kingdom / Jungle

You've been through a lot with no pity
Crushed on all sides in every city
As much as you create, they take
Treating your life and body
like an earthquake
Shaking your being to its tendons
No weapons for defending
Discounting your mind to their detriment
Why is it not your ending?
Father's words give you strength
Mother's love is your shield
Enslave ancestors bring us no shame
Grandma spoke purpose in your ear
Pawpaw gave immovable determination
The knowing of twenty thousand years
Rising cheers from an HBCU crowd
The world called you Hermes
You blushed,
owning the world
is not righteous
Through your brother's eyes
see all you are
No doubts left, you raised the bar
Damaged living beyond the scars
Strong beautiful like storms on Mars
Best of this world is seen
through your windows

You are a Snow
Born in the heat of the ghetto
Feeding off everything
your father didn't know
vitamins from my mother's strength
You have been to the wall
Congregating in pity with
brothers of the night's watch
Dedicated to the destruction
of someone else's assumption,
the fight is not at the wall
With a Malian straight sword
Cut down demon horde howling for my core
Block the slings and arrows of hate
With a Xhosa combat shield

Hardest battle fought is self-worth
Filled with the words of enemies
daggers pricking a million points on skin
Knock it down to your size
A new you appear
Quiet determination
Moving in tandem like dancing partners
Eyes spoke without words
Melancholy because you
forgotten more than you know
Scales fell from your eyes
Searing light penetrating revealing
the sons of ancestors radiating like
a living nuclear reactor
The true light of earth

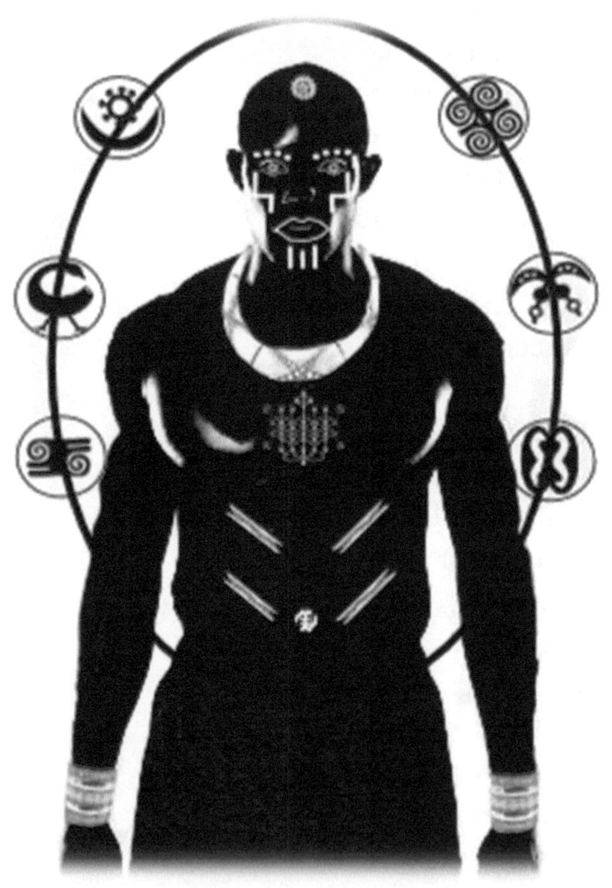

I'm here

Mannywellz /Peace

I am
Not going anywhere
My purpose is real
No less powerful
than your existence
When needed omnipotent
Not choked by toxic cis relationships
And ill-attended children
Given a million drops of blood
Stonewall in New York
water hoses in Birmingham
Here daily fighting the son of Sam
Enemy bullets blow holes in our chest
Talk, talk, talk tough, tough talk
When fascist assassins
start genocide part two

You see me now
When I was silent
you spit on me
Added more footprints
to my back
Told, you do not speak
or represent for us
In the name of James Baldwin,
Bessie Smith, Bayard Rustin,
Audre Lorde, Langston Hughes,
ninety percent of the Harlem Renaissance

black same gendered like me
You on some three-year-old
Daddy issues
Mad Dolomite, Pryor, and Brando
found out dick was alright
Not my fault
your hegemonic
demonic predilections
are a bust
Ain't got nothing to do with me
Headed out
Blowing up white supremacist activity
You in?
I love you
Need you
but spirit is losing breath
trying desperately
not to hold a grudge
based in karma

Religious Conversation

Kojey Radical / Pressure

God is your all in one
He whose dedication
means you throw away others
The one who makes the sun rise
Make heat dance an unrehearsed
Africa healing ritual
seeping into our cheeks
A path for you to walk
Riches of heaven imagined by man
captured on any artist's easel
Filled with despair deeper
than a child's double nightmare
Hope like a butterfly
flickering out of reach
between joy and peace
An impassable universe-wide chasm
beyond understanding, dangles hope

The voice of Bilal
bellows your daybreak
The soothing sound
of grandma's bedtime hymns
Angels watching over you
ushering to a future
guaranteed divine
Proverbs to curb action verbs
Temples built like castles
Testaments to your commitment

and prophesied reward
Scribed centuries before many cultures
Strength greater than a giant Zulu
stopped the sun for the dedicated
Perfect words from a god
without fault
Each night cherubim whisper
the prayers of children to Allah
They got it made, right?
Like a butterfly flickering out of reach
between joy and peace
An impassable universe-wide chasm
beyond understanding, dangles hope

Next Move

Dance Now/JID

Torn from the bosom
of the beginning
No more divine speech
Colors of life faded
into that drab life
Spirituals replaced
with regimented acts and
songs at the collection plate
Drum and call erased by
quiet supplications and
rare thigh slaps
Countries raped of souls
And the lands natural blood
Forced into amalgamations of cultures
still strong as hell
Making sense alone to
their engine of greed
Language like songs transliterated
to opera of the damned
Human capital traded or transported
everywhere but home
Aided and abetted extinction
of black-skinned people
Confusion and chaos left to rein
the energy of African peoples
Rip off the false European skins
Search ceaselessly for what you are
Back pressed to the wall

of white supremacy, religion,
and capitalism
In all your godliness
over-stand who's the sacrifice
then you know the next move
Back pressed up against the wall
by white supremacy, religion,
and capitalism
In all your godliness
over-stand who's the sacrifice
now what are you gon' do?

Wonder Why

Mereba/Planet U

Wonder why,
the lie
You scared now
Can't see a counter-narrative
Walk the world embarrassed
Change the lines of black existence
History of our people correcting itself
beyond CRT scare tactics
African continental mass
Larger than current maps
Black scares you deep
Balancing segregation and
blood on your soul
Gunpowder and steel
Brings you no closer to bliss
Trust in the privilege
and all it has taken
Good deeds burning at the altar
of your god won't save you
Spit in the face of the darkness
yet yearn to be indulged by it
Devour us down to our spirit
Desperate, disparate to dump
your sexual proclivities into
our magical bodies
Confiscate abuse our music magic
Even you know you can barely play it
Wonder why

We rebound no matter the
cancer-causing herbicide you use
Thriving beyond the pale of surviving
In truth, you wait like the fictional angels
to see what the first humans will do
Wonder why

Frequency

Donny Hathaway / What's Going On (Live)

Leave some pieces of the planet for us
trillions offered forever unsatiated
Crumbs of the earth are blood
Why make the world cry
My mind resonates
on an upper frequency
Drilling until the earth
bleeds black
pretty sapphires and diamonds
plucked from the mouths of
Tswana and Bantu
Love is a battlefield
Riddled with rape and incest
Anglo-Saxon is the culmination of
Germanic genes at their worst
You see the Windsor Elizabeth
The same inside and out
Trump the new euro hero
The smell of his ego and
narcissistic intentions
Feel like they in
Another dimension
Still taking boats
to pedo reef
Nothing Virgin
about the Island
Grabbing pussy
near ripping it out

Only way they'll get a baby
Blessed my mind resonates
on an upper frequency

Hallelujah, Back Children

Eric Roberson / First Love Jesus

Hallelujah black children
Moment you're born
racists start to labor
Fill your dreams with stones
False dogma hated Ethiop skin
Social media confirms they
wish it were theirs
Intelligent beyond compare
See the numbers of
darling obsidian geniuses
You bear no responsibility
for their fear
Or ushering them to humanity

Hallelujah black children
Stand on the tears of your elders
Forward facing
Elegba make the sweetest decision
at the crossroads
There is no value
I can place on a gift
we fully don't understand
how it comes to be
The fulfilled hopes
of the past generations
Even when I'm angry
my love shoves off the depth
Despite countless times
white supremacy dictated your ending
Live life fertilized by the love of the village
Trust in the future that you can conjure
Flex your creativity, it will keep you sane

Let us see your godly wonder

Hallelujah black children
Hallelujah amen.
Praise the lambs
whose mind is slaughtered
in schoolhouse
No sin is born to you
Belongs to the white man
We praise you
the objects of our love
The seat of our dreams
Bludgeoned by hate
You rise again speaking
With the wisdom they hate
Your laughter and joy,
Childhood games that echo
the future you seek
Hallelujah black children
Hallelujah amen.
You stand at the revival
Undoing our collective pain

Words…Are Bombs

Yasiin Bey (Mos Def)/Special Dedication

To shout, exhort my emotions
in a resounding drum call
Screeching raspy like
Bull Connor's words against
The progress of my people
Communication at its deepest
complex utterances of the soul
I attempt to sing verbs and
thoughts strung together tighter
than a gospel singer's felonious virginity
Make a body jerk and dance the day off

Inaudible
Inflection
Staccato word assault
Improvisation goads me to speak
divine meditation to the nations
Existing in the same time and space
Every time you hear me
crescendo off the back porch
Unafraid of the movements in this life
Your third eye smiles jazz

Jumping fences away from
the demonic cops
Streets know us, yet scared to see us become
Devouring soul spirituals
to spit more honest meanings

Holla but no one's listening
White teeth glistening
Cause some don't understand
Doesn't mean there's no
deep message in the broken English
A natural extension of the riotous poets
of the not-so-distant past
God, may she bless Gil Scott Heron
giving foundation to a new rhythm
Composed of the energy
from elders and ancestors
I be borrowing words
praying I could make new ones
Words are bombs
I fire at the enemy

Village Prayers

EARTHGANG/POWER

Blessings to the moon and star
Power in the collective meditation
Forging life with purpose
chain linked
Get the healer, your auntie
Cousin two miles over knows the way
Grandmother will divine the best day
Uncle has seen the stars fall
Herbs know your grandfather's wisdom
Tears of the father will help you see
My brothers' feet talk to the land
Sister plants seeds from
the roots of her hair
First born binds us all together
flowing through the fallopian tube
of our collective experiences
Listening for the first notes of life
Pathway to godhood is filled with blood
Shaping our crown so we receive the signal
Despite the distance to Alkebulan
you will see the way back
Rain down thousands of comets
on those who attempt
to thwart reigniting the power
of black consciousness
and revolutionary pursuits

Mdr kdrr
nna vnokk
Tdmk ntr

I speak a spell to empower you
I spit uhuru so you understand ubuntu
Asè

Two Bags of Sand

Joy Crookes/Since I Left You

Still moving despite
the weight of losing
Trying to make it past other grains
Some said my existence
in two lanes brought shame
Becoming the better me
arriving to my crown
Dropping out of warp factor eight
Shooting my double barrel
Klingon disruptor ray
I don't need Ooankali modifications
To be super, intelligent,
powerfully creative
Filled with wisdom
and ancient teachings
that sustained African people
for ten millennia
Two bags of sand balanced
oppression and resistance
Standing even when
knuckles drag the ground

True Religion

Nas/Nobody

You mentally deep
Strong on both feet
Spirit polished
with Ancestors whispers
Roads clear but never easy
Careful that's when the
white supremacists come for you
Religion keeps you broken
Vulnerable to mental suggestions
Osteen hid money in the holy uterus
Filled with the worst monsters
known all over the world
Destroying countries
under the lie of god's property
Subjugation of Africans for the dullard
Intimidated by black man's existence
Women perverted forced bludgeoned
to child factories
Non heterosexuals persecuted
thrown off Babel's porch
Epstein and Ghislaine book names priests
Speed dial to the papacy
Check caste system
Dalits under the foot of the Hindu
Allahu Akbar
Soldier your son and steal your daughter
They ain't all the same
yet the unholy permeates

all through you
I'll pass, won't screw you
Mixing energies is the end of me
instead, give them all an AIDS-infected dildo
Cultural and historical legacy
my true religion
Mentally deep
Olu's strong feet
Spirit polished
Ancestors' whispers
guide me

Super Alien

Ama Lou/Northside

Sometimes I wish I was a
super-powered alien
Annihilating the world's enemies
Dreaming about the death
of white supremacy
Rhe barbeque it
out of existence
Oshun's water
bring sphinx renewal

I get so tired of all the lying
People living zombified
middle-class congressman
drives a Maserati
Humans no longer
own humanity
Children deathly
pursue adulthood
Predators rape with
judicial accomplice
Billion-dollar war toys
given to Israel
Serving genocide
spiced with bitter apartheid
Trading souls
for economic gold
Same ones too lazy
to build their own

Whole world spitting
fascist hocus-pocus
Greedy African leaders
eat their people's spleen
I'm losing my black-conscious mind

Sometimes I wish I was a
super-powered alien
Annihilating the world's enemies
Mouth, watering over the death
of white supremacy
Rhe barbeque it out of existence
Oshun's water
bring no sphinx renewal

Same Ol' Slavery

Fantastic Negro/Nobody Makes Money

Erasure of all relevant data
from earth's servers
Blueprint to resolution
Of social-political issues
History reduced to memory
Aristotle stole the books
Shame in your soul because
you called us gods

Redistricting blacks
out of existence
No voice solving
white supremacist problems
Fear, just treatment is coming
to a theater near you
Our loyalty now is like
locating a goldilocks planet

Housing denied with the
advent of the middle class
City governments kept
the federal covenant
Blacks cannot buy their way
into the upper echelon
No place for us coincides
with America's dawn

Land stabilizes a
family generationally
it gives an indelible ink
sense of permanence
A cursory glance at
the black farmer's life
is plenty evidence
of anti-black disenfranchisement
Hands out to Olu
praying for more
than subsistence

Healthcare perfected procedures
on African women
Profiting off vaccinations
from Henrietta Lacks DNA
Learned long ago
they'll monetize your soul
Reason why we struggle
to grow old

Black conservative,
new name for Tom
Sell out their people
at Wall Street's closing bell
Hoping to be
grafted into whiteness
At spaceship launch
the only seat is
beneath a racist's feet

I Don't Lie to Africans

Juls / No Lie

No lie
African
the first formed
from the ethereal mist
and particulate
Willing yourself
to become
this planet isn't
worth cultivating
without you
Best of all beginnings
was touched by you
An ancient mage speaking
the unbelievable
from your fingers
You have no accountability
to their code
Confess the forty-two
Maat is in the booth
No lie
African
No lie

No lie
Lust for what you are
Desecrated your
history cities temples
Erased books

Fear of black power
had them cowering
in the shadow of caves
No lie
No lie
No lie African
the first God
White supremacy
hate this truth
Copy and paste
does not work on us
Our DNA permeates
Blessed assurance to our
permanent existence
Stand and look into their eyes
without fear
They have always cowered
in the presence of light
I feed you these adjectives
Not to inflame your heart
A whisper of music
to awaken your joy

No lie

Hermes Protocol II
Isaiah Rashad/Headshots (4 Da Locals)

Black and beautiful as a mufukka
Inside and out
that's why they hate a lot
Original scientists inventing reason
Engineering the first cities
How to keep homes cool
Chartered stars and the planets
Colonizers remain confused
Since BCE started stealing ideas
It's the reason for the situation right here
Don't let the current
keep you dismayed
Karma and the planet
Reshaping that future fake
Walk the streets with swagger
Beings filled with juju
Mold yourself back together

When they saw you
remarkable intelligence
New gods come the black skins
Sat at your feet
Socrates had no shame
Searching for knowledge
ask the nearest black man
Built oases from the upper kingdom
to Mauritania
Preoccupied with the better

Not ultimate creations of world death
Annihilation of culture
and history of a people not us
first definitions of society
Uhuru we all in together
The current state
is a not a mustard seed
in the field of our existence
Karma and the planet
Reshaping that future fake
Walk the streets with swagger
Beings filled with juju
Mold yourself back together

God

EARTHGANG /AMEN

Get down on your knees to me
Get down on your knees to me
Get down on your knees to me
I did when my mother
kept rats from eating me

I don't give a damn for your love
No prerequisite for my manna
Be there more times than Yahweh
He's too busy looking at the sparrows
Your eyes I will clean with my tears
Best decisions are seen
Strengthen your body
so, you move swiftly
Feed your inner universe
with quantum-level molecules
Build a world where you flourish
readying for the eventual space odyssey
Then come live amongst us
Get full off the collective godhood

Get down on your knees to me
Get down on your knees to me
Get down on your knees to me
I did when my mother
kept rats from eating me

Now it's simple to share in
the same time and space
Healing each other's disease
and aches
Loving one another
like a slice peace cobbler
and slow-churn ice cream
Living great great-daddy's waking dream
Ancient mother waving a kente cloth
dabbing her eyes in joy
Y'all must have kissed the Atum-Rhe
You know where all the stars are unseen
This is how I get my rocks off
Filled with immeasurable elation
Your scars have become
your birthmark
Euphoric spiritual ejaculation
Immaculate creation is the pathway
Crowns all around
Better than backing it up
and bussing it open
I beg you gods,
be odd so you can be seen

Get down on your knees to me
Get down on your knees to me
Get down on your knees to me
I did when my mother
kept two rats from eating me

Sango's Spell / Defund the Police

Christian Scott aTunde Adjuah/Double Consciousness

When it began, we all knew it was the end…
He was riding the bus home
The same group of tired souls
gathered and swaying in the
exhaust fumes and bad breaks.
Listening to a mix of jazz and hip-hop
his star-child brother created
He appreciated the concern
the understanding
Sharing of dreams
and disappointment
Strips of fried sun rays
and coffee with grits
The way you support your family
Every point in the beat is important
Each song on the list
a phrase of a love letter
The music helped him see his people
Instead of drowning them
in simple Simon rhythms

Interruptions are our daily vitamins
Blaring sirens and frenetic pale
comparisons to heavens lights
Bus pulled over
great mother in the back
pulling out her beads
Jehovah Jireh time for a

righteous salve of medicine
Doors busted open and protector
adorned in mech suits
Stomped the floor harder
than black frats on the yard
We need ID from all
who fits the description
He stood up
IDs are useless cause
black life doesn't matter
Black boy yanked by his collar
Tossed like a mangy dog
against the rail
Laughter stopped
among the troops
under the black boy's
steaming saliva
He had already prayed
In deep fear anger and rage
spiritual exhaustion in step with
I shall not be moved

Sango, Sango, Sango
Give me your fire
Sango, Sango, Sango
give me your fire
To burn away the light
and bring back the darkness
Sango, I mount you
and take your power
Devour those who steal
our flowers
And replace them

with viruses filled bulbs
Sango give *me* your fire

The protectors could feel
the pressure changing
The front of the bus
exploded outward
An eight-year-old black girl
smiling, resting her chin
on the back of her hands,
Go do your thing big bro
She laughed and so did the others
His arm glowed bright orange
to pale blue up to his elbow
Then a flash of fire traversed ten feet
in point zero seconds
His right fist touched
the protector's armor
It sailed backward
out the front window
Sonic boom, ash and smoke
heat dissipated
Crater like a football field
and crumbling bones
was all we could see

Leaping from the bus
thirty feet into the air
He landed like a dove
beyond the crater
Reminiscent of the hole
in the heart of this country
So, we followed

We all followed his path
toward the citadel that dispatches
Spartans on you and me
A million purpose-filled
black men duty bound
to put down the hellhounds
The driving drum rhythm
all-spark in his heart
He struck the ground
and a firenado, pregnant
with a black woman's
tears and anguish
cleansed the land of
the most stubborn evil
Cut and paste the same like
racist do with redistricting
'Til the country was purified
in Lake Minnetonka
I shall not be moved

Sango, Sango, Sango
Give me your fire
Sango, Sango, Sango
give me your fire
To burn away the light
and bring back the darkness
Sango, I mount you
and take your power
Devour those who
steal our flowers
And replace them
with viruses filled bulbs
Sango give me your fire

ACKNOWLEDGEMENTS

Writing the books was harder than I thought, given I have published other works. None of this would have been possible without my mother. She always encourages me to write since I was a child, first writing incoherent sentences and stories. I also want to acknowledge my friend Dwayne Smith, whose renewed friendship has inspired and built confidence.

I also want to thank my partner, Chris, for putting up with me as a polymath who is always working on something and is patient in the middle of other issues in our lives. I hope you see it now!

I'm profoundly grateful to Louis Cross, a mentor who took time from his wife and kids to make sure the black boy of someone he was not related to understand the opportunities around him and that I am as capable as anyone in my sphere. It is a beautiful thing for black men to care for children who are not their own. A true alpha male in the manner!

To my brother Earl, who constantly tells me to not be afraid of words and reassures me that this is our time as conscientious black men and women to be heard for the better of our people.

Writing these poems to address various personal or world social-political issues has been a soul-searching task in all honesty and love for myself and the desire for us to be mentally free. I'm indebted to my editors for all their work and effort to ensure that the thoughts outweighed anything else so that what is presented is along the lines of what is needed at this time.

To my family: for always being the people I could turn to during those dark and desperate times of this life. They have sustained me in ways I never knew I needed. Many of these same issues or stories are also part of who you are. I'm so thankful to have you back in my life. Thank you all for helping me get here!

Orlando Taylor is the author of many poems in several anthologies, such as his previous work, *My Scars Are My Birthmark, Blues Arrival: Stories of the Queer Black South and Migrations*, and online poetry blog sites. He is currently working on several films, television, and print ideas.

PLAYLIST QR CODE

www.ingramcontent.com/pod-product-compliance
Lightning Source LLC
Chambersburg PA
CBHW020047310726
48970CB00007B/2454